READING POWER

European Colonies in the Americas

Spanish Colonies in the Americas

Lewis K. Parker

The Rosen Publishing Group's
PowerKids Press™
New York

Published in 2003 by The Rosen Publishing Group, Inc.
29 East 21st Street, New York, NY 10010

First Edition

Book Design: Erica Clendening

Photo Credits: Cover © Art Resource, NY; p. 4 Erica Clendening; pp. 5, 6, 7, 8–9, 10, 11, 13, 14–15, 16–17 © North Wind Picture Archives; p. 15 Rosen Publishing; pp. 18–19 Photo Collection, Los Angeles Public Library; pp. 20–21 © Bill Varie/Corbis

Library of Congress Cataloging-in-Publication Data

Parker, Lewis K.
Spanish colonies in the Americas / Lewis K. Parker.
    v. cm. — (European colonies in the Americas)
Includes bibliographical references and index.
Contents: Spain takes on the world — Hernan Cortes and the Aztecs — Francisco Pizarro and the Incas — Junipero Serra and the missions — Presidios and pueblos — Spain's other colonies.
ISBN 0-8239-6471-X (lib. bdg.)
1. America—Discovery and exploration—Spanish—Juvenile literature.
2. Spain—Colonies—America—History—Juvenile literature. 3.
Explorers—America—History—Juvenile literature. 4.
Explorers—Spain—History—Juvenile literature. 5.
Spaniards—America—History—Juvenile literature. [1. America—Discovery and exploration—Spanish. 2. Spain—Colonies—America. 3.
Spaniards—America—History. 4. Frontier and pioneer life. 5. United States—History—Colonial period, ca. 1600-1775.] I. Title.
E123 .P33 2003
980'.013—dc21

                                        2002000129

Contents

The Search for Gold

About 500 years ago, Spain was a rich and very powerful nation. However, Spain wanted more wealth. After Christopher Columbus discovered the Americas, Spain sent more explorers to find gold and silver there.

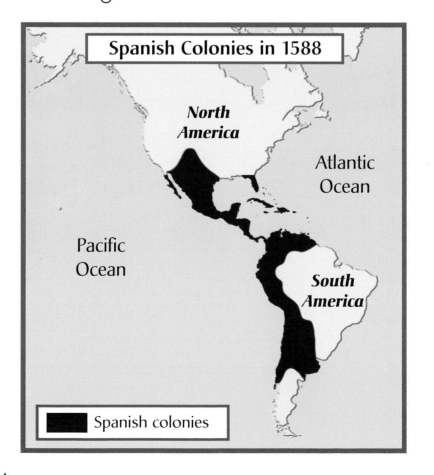

Spanish Colonies in 1588

North America

Atlantic Ocean

Pacific Ocean

South America

◼ Spanish colonies

In 1492, King Ferdinand II and Queen Isabella of Spain paid for Columbus's trip to the Americas.

Cortés and Pizarro

Hernán Cortés *(ehr-NAN kor-TEHZ)* was a Spanish explorer. In 1519, he and 600 men sailed from Cuba to Mexico. Native people called Aztecs had a great nation in Mexico. In 1521, Cortés overthrew the Aztecs and claimed Mexico as a colony of Spain. He forced the Aztecs to work in gold and silver mines. He sent the riches back to Spain.

Cortés was the first European to discover the southern part of California.

Cortés meets the Aztec ruler

The Incas were natives of South America. They lived in Peru. Like the Aztecs, the Incas also had a great nation. In 1532, Francisco Pizarro *(fruhn-SIS-koh puh-ZAR-oh)* and about 200 soldiers set off from Panama for Peru. Pizarro had heard that there was a lot of gold in Peru.

Pizarro took control of the Incas and their gold. He sent the gold back to Spain.

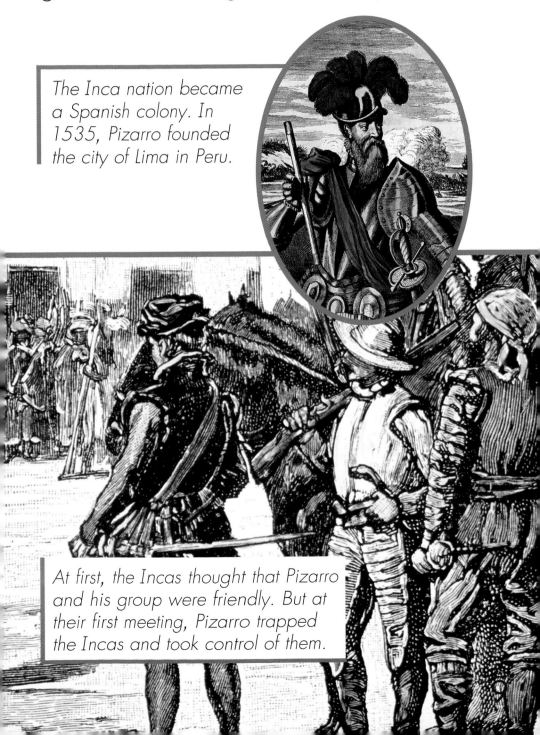

The Inca nation became a Spanish colony. In 1535, Pizarro founded the city of Lima in Peru.

At first, the Incas thought that Pizarro and his group were friendly. But at their first meeting, Pizarro trapped the Incas and took control of them.

Missions, Presidios, and Pueblos

The people in Spain felt their church was very important. They wanted the native people in their colonies to share their religious beliefs. Beginning in the 1760s, Spain set up missions in its North American colonies to teach its religion to Native Americans. Father Junípero Serra *(hoo-NEE-peh-roh SEHR-uh)* started the first nine missions in California.

Father Serra's Missions

San Diego (1769)
San Carlos Borromeo (1770)
San Antonio (1771)
San Gabriel (1771)
San Luis Obispo (1772)
San Francisco (1776)
San Juan Capistrano (1776)
Santa Clara (1777)
San Buenaventura (1782)

Father Junípero Serra

A mission included a church, workshops, and houses. These buildings were often made from clay bricks. Native Americans lived and worked at the missions.

Mission San Luis Obispo, today

Native Americans received religious lessons at the missions.

15

To keep the missions safe, the Spanish built forts called presidios. Presidios were used by soldiers.

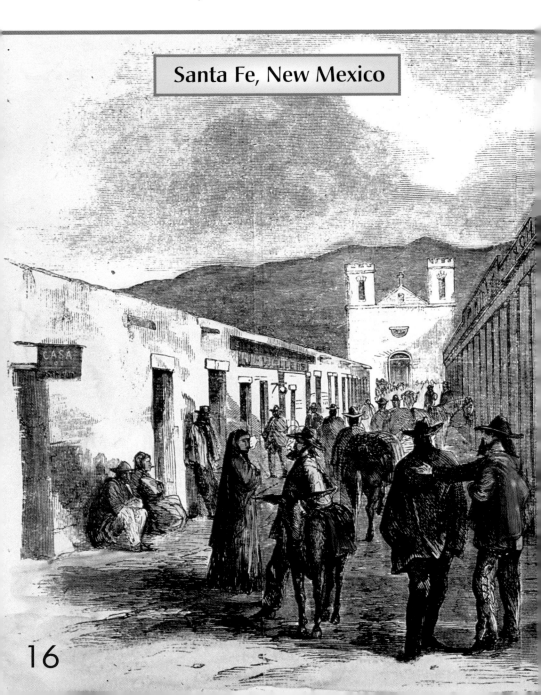

Santa Fe, New Mexico

Outside the presidios, towns called pueblos were built. Spanish settlers came to live in the pueblos.

Santa Fe, New Mexico, was used as an army and missionary base by the Spanish. Santa Fe is the oldest capital city in the United States.

In 1777, the first pueblo in California was built. It was called San Jose. Three years later, the pueblo that became the city of Los Angeles was started. By 1820, about 650 people lived in Los Angeles.

Los Angeles, 1857

Los Angeles started as a small settlement of only 46 people. By the 1850s, there were about 4,000 people living in Los Angeles. Today, over 9.5 million people live in Los Angeles.

The End of Spain's Colonies

By the early 1800s, Spain began to lose control of its colonies in the Americas. In 1819, the United States bought Florida. In 1821, Mexico became its own country.

In 1850, California became a part of the United States.

Today, many people who live in the places that were once Spanish colonies speak the Spanish language and follow many Spanish practices. Spain's colonies have left a lasting mark on life in the Americas.

TIME LINE

1492–1502	Columbus discovers the Americas.
1521	Cortés overthrows the Aztecs.
1533	Pizarro overthrows the Incas.
1565	St. Augustine is founded.
1598	The New Mexico colony is founded.
1769	Father Serra starts his first mission.
1777	The first pueblo in California at San Jose is founded.
1819	Florida is sold to the United States.
1821	Mexico is no longer a colony of Spain.
1850	California becomes a U.S. state.

Los Angeles, California, today

Glossary

Americas (uh-**mehr**-uh-kuhz) the name used when speaking about North America, South America, and Central America

capital (**kap**-uh-tuhl) the main city of a government

colony (**kahl**-uh-nee) a faraway land that belongs to or is under the control of a nation

explorer (ehk-**splor**-uhr) a person who searches for new places

fort (**fort**) a strong building or place that can be guarded easily

mission (**mish**-uhn) a place where the work of church groups is carried on

presidios (prih-**see**-dee-ohz) military forts

pueblo (**pwehb**-loh) a Spanish village or town

religion (rih-**lihj**-uhn) belief in a god and the practice of praying to that god

religious (rih-**lihj**-uhs) having to do with a god or a system of faith

wealth (**wehlth**) a great amount of riches

Resources

Books

The Travels of Hernan Cortés
by Deborah Crisfield
Raintree Steck-Vaughn Publishers (2000)

The California Missions
by Elizabeth Van Steenwyck
Franklin Watts (1998)

Web Sites

Due to the changing nature of Internet links, PowerKids Press has developed an online list of Web sites related to the subjects of this book. This site is updated regularly. Please use this link to access the list:

http://www.powerkidslinks.com/euca/spa/

Index

Word Count: 431

Note to Librarians, Teachers, and Parents

If reading is a challenge, Reading Power is a solution! Reading Power is perfect for readers who want high-interest subject matter at an accessible reading level. These fact-filled, photo-illustrated books are designed for readers who want straightforward vocabulary, engaging topics, and a manageable reading experience. With clear picture/text correspondence, leveled Reading Power books put the reader in charge. Now readers have the power to get the information they want and the skills they need in a user-friendly format.

DATE DUE

JAN 0 2 2007